How Privacy Keeps You From

Tindering:

To swipe or not to swipe!

By: Sandra Odisho

Acknowledgments

I would like to express my greatest admiration for the wonderful people who made this book happen. I would first of all like to thank Professor Olena Kobzar for all her dedication and hard work in helping me prepare for this piece. She has been a wonderful contribution in helping learn more about different privacy policies and how they come about, but also believing in me as a student. I would also like to thank Behzad Mohammad for pushing me to reach my full potential and helping me do better. Finally, I would like to thank Robert Valvasori and Celeste Pellicore for all the editing that was done to help make this a wonderful piece.

Table of Contents

The social media that was chosen to be critique is Tinder. With over 50 million users, Tinder is popular due to the fact that people are able to meet their "significant other" who lives merely a few kilometers away from them. Originally, Tinder was intended for people to meet and get to know each other, since they are always in a rush, but it slowly came to be known as an application where people could hook up. This explains the little fire as Tinder's logo, which is seen as a way to ignite kindling. This elucidates how the symbol on Tinder (fire) represents the forming of a relationship and as the fire is burning it represents the chemistry between the two people. Once the fire dies down, the couple is finally aware of whom the other person really is and where the relationship is leading, which either can be good or bad, dependent on the relationship. However, although Tinder is a way for people to connect, its privacy policy depicts a framework in which people should be much more aware of whom they are getting to know. Taking precaution on any social media is an important factor with respect to staying safe online and making sure that no one is being harmed. Examining Tinder's Privacy policy is important to understand how Tinder tries to protect people when they are online. While we may blame Tinder for all inadequate knowledge that is provided to us, it is important to mention that people who are not taking the initiative and making themselves aware of the privacy policy can dictate why many peoples' privacy gets violated. Although PIPEDA is a legislation that tries to protect Canadians in terms of online privacy, it will be argued that it is too narrow and inadequate to meet the current fast pace challenges of technology and the fast pace growth of social media. What was emerging in 2004 in terms of social media is different from what is happening now in 2016 because social media continues to evolve to meet the demand of society as well as the market. Tinder may be one form of social media, but their privacy policy will depict a larger picture of whether or not it protects Canadians as a whole. It is important to look at the privacy policy of Tinder and whether their privacy is, in fact, private. The latest terms of use that will be looked at is of July 31, 2015, although there may be previous versions for this application. This paper will start off with the general description of the application and then go on to talk about the privacy information that Tinder sets out for its users. Next, we look at how Tinder through PIPEDA and deconstruct it by looking at how PIPEDA is problematic. Finally, this paper will look at safeguards and solutions that can be created to better assist Tinder by trying to safeguard their users' private information and how PIPEDA can be modified so that it can still be applicable to all social media platforms.

General

Tinder states that they respect the privacy of their users and through this idea they developed its privacy policy by demonstrating their commitment to protecting our privacy and also respecting their users' privacy; however, by doing so it was the only way for Tinder to operate. This privacy policy describes all the information that Tinder collects, how that information is used and with whom it is shared. Although it is common that we do not read Tinder's privacy policy, it is encouraged by the developers to read it carefully when using their application or when we have business with them so that we are aware of what they are offering to us and what we are sharing with them. When we use Tinder, we are informally accepting everything stated in their privacy policy, whether we like it or not. If we do not accept the privacy policy, then we are unable to use their application.

Generally, Tinder is allowed to collect information that can identify their user, which includes the person's personal information such as their name, email address along with other information that can identify them. Tinder can collect our information through their website or a mobile application by the user. When deciding to use Tinder, we authorize the application to gather and retain data related to the application. This means that whatever a person does on the application is shared with Tinder because when we sign up we have given them consent to collect whatever information we wish to provide to them. We should question whether or not the consent we decided to give Tinder was the user actually approving with everything Tinder stated in their privacy policy. When we provide our personal information through their service, the information we share gets sent out to servers in the United States, but also to countries all over the world to develop this data double. Data double is explained as a virtual self that is more authentic than the real life self. The virtual right has no legal right and it is hard to know when or what kind of harm if any has occurred.[1]

Overview

---

[1] Kobzar, Olena. "Introducing the Data Double." Lecture.

When we first sign up for Tinder, we are asked to connect to Facebook in order to use the application. This is one of the problems that come up because Tinder should not be connected to Facebook, but instead we should use an email address of our choosing or create an account without the use of Facebook. Many people post personal information on Facebook for family and friends to see and using an application like Tinder can affect the person negatively depending on what they decide to post on Facebook. Once we sign onto Facebook, we authorize Tinder to access certain Facebook information, such as our profile picture, email address, gender, birthday, education, relationship interests - male or female- current city, personal description, friends list including information along with photos of our Facebook friends who might be common Facebook friends with other Tinder users. Once we are in, Tinder asks us to allow our location information from our device to be accessed when we download or use the application. Having our location enabled while using Tinder is dangerous in terms of safety concerns for individuals as well as anyone who uses the application because anyone is able to locate where you live, work or go to school. Furthermore, having the location enabled is not actually maximizing the full potential of the user to meet other people

because it can put someone in a dangerous situation. It may seem as

if the application is trying to maximize the full potential of their

services for the user, but it really is doing the opposite. Do we need

to have our location enabled to connect to people on Tinder or can

we just connect people based on interests or education? Tinder

should not allow people to use their location to a very close

proximity through distance, but rather just the city. By doing so,

people who do not feel compelled to expose their location to other

people are not obligated too. Furthermore, if a person decides to

share some of their information with another user, it is because the

person decided to do it based on their own discretion. Tinder may

also collect and store any personal information we provide while

using their services such as our name, address, email address and

telephone number. While using Tinder, we are also able to provide

them with photos through Facebook, a personal description of us,

and information about our gender and preferences for

recommendations such as distance, age range, and gender. When we

chat with other users, we provide Tinder with the content of our

chats and if we contact them with a customer service or other inquiry, we provide them with the content of the conversation. It is interesting to note that although Tinder saves all of our conversations, they rarely respond to customers who have questions or feedback. We can now ask are we really safe with an application where they do not care about the safety of their own users. One problem that arose when someone contacted Tinder was when a girl emailed the application headquarters and told them that someone was using her pictures as a way to spam other people. The only time Tinder responded to this girl was not even remotely helpful because they stated that each Tinder profile is tied to a unique Facebook account and she should contact Facebook's help center to file a report.[2] It seemed as if Tinder did not care about the girl's privacy and the girl was left with a creepy experience, in which she realized that Tinder is not as safe as they say they are.[3] Nothing a person does online is safe, but it is recommended by Tinder to take extra precaution to safeguard our personal information.

When a person creates a Tinder account, the person has the ability to review and update their personal information within Tinder

---

[2] McCarthy, Kelly. "Someone Used My Photo to Create a Fake Tinder Account, And It Could Happen to You."
[3] IBID.

by accessing their settings tab. There is only one way to delete your account and that is through the settings page on the person's account. Once the account is closed, Tinder will continue to retain certain information that is associated with the users' account for analytical purposes and recordkeeping integrity, as well as to prevent fraud from occurring. This seems like a positive thing Tinder is doing, but what the important to remember is that Tinder will always retain your information forever, instead of getting rid of it after a few days. Our private information that we decided to share at the time, should have been kept for recordkeeping purposes as long as we were using Tinder, but as soon as we deactivated the account, there is no need for our information to be saved somewhere in the online world for others to have access to. Tinder tries to enforce their terms of use on their users, take actions that they assume is necessary to protect the integrity of their service or their users and also take other actions that are considered admissible by law. Furthermore, if certain information has already been provided to third parties, it is assumed that the information which has been provided will be subject to those third parties' privacy policies and not Tinder. This means that Tinder's privacy policy is different from other third party applications and we should not assume that what is applied to Tinder would be applied to any other third party application and vice versa.

Third party applications that Tinder is associated with are other Match groups, which as of July 31, 2015; include websites and applications such as Ourtime.com, BlackPeopleMeet.com, OkCupid, Match, and HowAboutWe. By using Tinder, we are authorizing anything from our personal and non-personal information to be sent to other Match businesses, business partners and other third parties to have access to. This violates principle 7 of PIPEDA about safeguards because the person has his/her information shared with other groups, in which that information may be private and personal. Why do websites such as OkCupid or blackpeoplemeet need our information if we do not plan on using that site? These online dating sites do not need to obtain and keep our personal information for their own personal gain when there is a higher chance that one might not use that website, especially if a person had a bad experience with one dating site. Should these sites be allowed to just go in and take our information unwillingly to see what our interest may include? That would be inaccurate because, in order to keep people safe, Tinder should allow their users to either accept or reject whether they want their information shared with other match groups. Tinder does state who our personal information is shared too, but it does not state what those companies do with our personal information. Also, it does not state if those companies ever destroy any information that they receive from Tinder after a while. Furthermore, in the privacy policy, Tinder states that they do share our personal information with other sites (aside from the applications stated such as OKCupid or Blackpeoplemeet.com) that is not directly stated in their privacy policy. Tinder collects any and all credit card information when you decide to purchase in-app services such as additional swipes.

When we visit Tinder, we can assign our device one or more cookies to enable or allow access for Tinder to obtain and personalize our experience. Cookies are small files which are stored on a user's computer and are designed to hold a certain amount of data specific to a particular client and website and can be accessed either by the web server or the client computer.[4] This allows the server to deliver a page tailored to a particular user, or the page itself can contain some script which is aware of the data in the cookie and

---

[4] Are Cookies? Computer Cookies Explained."

so it is able to carry information from one visit to the website (or related site) to the next.[5]

Tinder is able to automatically collect information about our activity on their services, such as the pages we visit, time and date of our visits and the links we click. If we advertise Tinder on Facebook or other websites, then Tinder may use certain data collected on their service to show us their own advertisements on other websites or applications. This is very relevant when using Facebook because, from past experience, a Facebook advertisement is often asking people to join Tinder. Additionally, Tinder has also embedded pixel tags (also called web beacons or clear GIFs) on web pages, advertisements, and emails, which are tiny, invisible graphics that are used to access cookies and track our activities. Cookies track our activity based on how many pages are viewed and around what time they are viewed. This goes against our privacy right to do what we want online because every site that we go to gets tracked by Tinder, which gives them information about what we search and how many times a day or week we go to a specific website. It is not about hiding what we do online, but Tinder is also tracking what we search

---

[5] Are Cookies? Computer Cookies Explained."

on google and after taking Privacy and the Law, it is clear that people do weird things online and we would prefer to keep some things private. There is an explosive power to secrets and it is only dangerous when it is made public.[6] Melanie McGuire also known as the suitcase killer googled "how to commit murder" right before killing her husband and since googling things online is not private, it is seen as evidence, but also for the public to view. [7]

When we use Tinder with our mobile device we are given a unique identifier assigned to our device by the manufacturer instead of obtaining cookies, which is able to recognize a person. Tinder does this to store our preferences and track our use of the application in case we ever return to it, but also for their own record. How are we supposed to use an application that is aware of everything we are doing without evening consenting to it? Our consent is important and it can be seen as a legal binding document/agreement between two people about a code of conduct. For example, the application versus the user and how they should act. A case that was prominent was about a man named Gable Tostee who was charged with the murder

---

[6] Kobzar, Olena. Secrets. Lecture 11
[7] Epstein, Sue. "Convicted Suitcase Killer Melanie McGuire Is Investigating If Her Lawyer Was on Drugs during Her 2007 Trial."

of Warriena Wright.[8] The police were able to arrest the man by

going through his matches and talking to them to see if they had

come into contact with him.[9] Police said on the night the pair met,

after purchasing alcohol they returned to Tostee's apartment where

toxicology reports revealed wright also consumed a quantity of

home distilled white spirits.[10] After they had sex which was recorded

on Tostee's mobile phone, there was an altercation that included

Wright's breathing becoming restricted as she was restrained and she

was pleading to be allowed to leave the property, but Tostee forced

her onto the balcony.[11] Although our privacy is infringed upon,

having our information monitored can be beneficial in solving a case

or helping out a person in trouble. Unlike cookies, the device ID

cannot be deleted, but Advertising IDs can be reset in "Settings" on

our IPhones. If a person does not own an IPhone, then they are

unable to do anything about it. Advertisement companies also use

these device IDs or Advertising IDs to track our use of the app, track

the number of advertisements displayed, measure advertisement

---

[8] Moir, Jo. "Tinder Helps Build Case."
[9] IBID.
[10] IBID.
[11] IBID.

performance and display advertisements that are more relevant to the user.

Tinder may allow service providers, advertising companies, and advertised networks along with other third party members to display their own advertisements on Tinder. These companies are able to use tracking technologies, such as cookies or embedded pixel tags to collect information about users who are viewing or interacting with their advertisements. Tinder is able to share non-personal information about us that they collect with other Match Group companies and other third party groups to develop specific advertisements on their Service and on websites or applications of third parties (e.g. Facebook, Instagram, and Twitter). This way Tinder can combine non-personal information with additional non-personal information collected from other sources. Furthermore, opting out of Tinder will not decrease the number of advertisements a person sees on other websites that they go on. According to PIPEDA, this violates principle 4 about limiting collection because the collection of our personal information has not been limited to what the organization is saying, but rather it is shared with other third parties and other organizations that store our information for future purposes. Tinder should limit the disclosure of any personal information they may have so that the privacy of their users are protected.

How does Tinder use the information they collect about us? Tinder states that they collect information about us to improve their products and services, but also to manage their business. They are able to manage our account and provide us with customer support, perform research and analysis about our use of Tinder, and communicate with users in several ways such as email, telephone or mobile devices about products or services that may be interesting to us. This can be done either through Tinder or accessing other third parties associated with Tinder. Tinder can also develop, display, and track content and advertising tailored to our interests on their service and other websites, including providing their advertisements to us when we visit other websites. It is interesting to note that although Tinder states that they would communicate with us by email or telephone about any questions or issues we have, they do not get back to a person unless it is a technical issue with the application as a whole, in which most times a person is unable to sign in because it either automatically logs them out or the site crashes. Furthermore, they do not look into the privacy aspect of the application and they do not answer any questions regarding problems a user may face with their privacy policy, especially if you are arguing against it. Another significant problem is that they do not have a number to contact them, which means that you are forced to email them, in which they do not need to respond, but only send you a confirmation email that they received it. Once you send them an email you receive a page that says "thank you for contacting us, we will get back to you shortly." This is vague because there is no definite timeframe of when they would get back to the person.

When we submit our personal information to apply for a job with Tinder, the information that we provide for them can include our name, contact information, prior education, and experience, which is shared with third party service providers. This information can be retained by them to collect, maintain and analyze the candidate for the job postings. Tinder may perform these functions directly or use a third party application to perform these functions on our behalf who are obligated to use our personal information only to perform services for them. Furthermore, if we access our service from a third party social platform, such as Facebook, Tinder may share non-personal information with Facebook to a certain extent, depending on how we have set our privacy settings on Facebook. When we are on Facebook we can change the settings so that people do not know we use Tinder, but regardless of changing the settings, the application still takes all our information and stores it. A problem that arises is that we did not authorize for Facebook to collect information about what we are doing on Tinder, but since we allowed it, we have no control over it and if we say "no", then we are unable to use the application. Either way, our privacy does become infringed upon whether we like it or not and this question whether Tinder is safe or not. The information being shared on Tinder can violate principle 6 of PIPEDA about accuracy because not all information we share can be accurate and it does not mean that we are actually telling the truth on the application.

Who does Tinder Share our information with? Our information is shared with other users on the application and when we register; our profile becomes visible and viewable by other users of the service. The information we provide will be viewed by other Tinder users because we have allowed it to happen directly through Facebook. This goes against our privacy to hide who we are from strangers because as a safety concern, people do not want some random stranger knowing where they go to school or how far they are from them. It would not be surprising if people were getting "stalked" by someone due to Tinder's Privacy. If two people swipe right, you get a connection and those two people can now start chatting, but if only one person swipes left, then the two people do not match and they are not able to talk to one another. If you chat with your match, then your match can see the content of the chat; however, even if a person does not match with you, they are still able to access your information that is on your profile. If you do not want someone to know who you are, then why can Tinder not find a way to change the settings to still make a profit for the company, but also be a safety mechanism for users. As a previous user of Tinder, it has come to my attention that you either end up with a good experience according to what Tinder's privacy policy states or a scary experience due to its privacy.

Tinder states that it does not share our personal information with others except for what is stated in their privacy policy or when they inform us of any changes they make so that we have the opportunity to opt out of having our personal information shared.

Tinder may share our personal and financial information with service providers and that gives these service providers access to our personal information that is needed to perform certain functions but is not allowed to share or use this information for any other purpose, which can include online dating websites. For example, Tinder's new update has super likes where after a certain amount of swipes you have the option of making a payment and you can receive unlimited likes. Furthermore, this means that these service providers can disclose our personal information to whomever they want too. The person's credit card information is saved and stored for future purposes. It is important to ask: why does Tinder need our credit card information? All our personal and financial information is on our credit cards and if a company like Tinder has access to it, we are giving away our right to keep our financial information private. A users' information – personal or financial – is retained for as long as Tinder needs and they are able to share it with third parties if the third party asks for it. Even if a user decides to delete their account before Tinder decides to change their privacy policy, the user's information is still relevant to the new policy, even though the user is not using the application anymore. In certain cases, Tinder may raise or waive any legal objection or right available to us because they believe that disclosure is appropriate only when trying to investigate, prevent, or take other action regarding illegal activity, suspected fraud or other wrongdoings to protect and defend the rights, property or safety of their company, employees, users or third parties. This is stating that Tinder can share our information with third parties, but not to its users. The company is clearly looking out for its best interest and not protecting their users' privacy rights.

Do Not Track ("DNT") is a privacy preference that users can set in their web browsers and it is a way for users to inform websites and services that they do not want certain information about their webpage visits collected over time and across websites or online services. Firstly, it can be guaranteed that no person on Tinder actually uses "DNT" because they may be unaware of this option, and secondly, whether we use DNT or not, it does not guarantee that Tinder will not be using our personal information for their own gain or obtain our information through other ways. Thirdly, Tinder never informed their users about this privacy preference and although it is stated in their privacy policy, it was placed in the middle of the document towards the end, where it is common knowledge that people would not actually read the whole thing. According to Tinder's privacy policy, they are committed to providing us with meaningful choices about the information they collect and that is why they provide the opt-out links; however, although this may seem like a benefit towards the user, Tinder does not recognize or respond to any DNT signals as the internet industry is working towards trying to define what exactly DNT means. The problem is that the internet industry does not know what it means to comply with DNT or have a common approach to responding to DNT. Why would we apply DNT to Tinder, if it is not possible for Tinder to comply with it themselves? Tinder cannot expect its users to follow the rules, web they do not follow the rules themselves. Even though we have DNT, it is clear Tinder is violating principle 1 of PIPEDA because they are trying to not be held accountable for their actions by claiming one thing and doing another through DNT. Since Lawyers must remember that they remain accountable for information transferred to third parties for processing, the same thing should be applied to Tinder.

There are many places on Tinder where a person can click on a link to access other websites that do not operate under Tinder's privacy policy. This is also known as spam and if we click on an advertisement through Tinder, then we may be taken to a website that Tinder or the use of the application does not control. These third-party websites may independently solicit and collect our personal information and in some instances, provide the third party website with information about our activities on those websites. Although we did not authorize this directly, we are forced to follow their privacy policy. Tinder recommends that we refer back to the privacy statements of all third-party websites we visit by clicking on the "privacy" link typically located at the bottom of the webpage we are visiting. This is a problem because realistically a person does not have time to read through the countless pages of privacy policies and it would seem time-consuming.

What choices do we have about Tinder collecting and using our information? As a Tinder user, we do have the option to not provide Tinder with certain information, but that may result in us being unable to use certain features on their service because certain information is required for us to register as a user. One thing that was constantly discussed was the connecting of Facebook, but also, if we do not pay for certain functions then we cannot use them. Also, the location is another problem because we have to make sure we enable the location in order to use the application. Tinder can deliver notifications to our phones and we can disable these notifications at any time by going into "app settings" or by changing the setting on our phone, which seems like a benefit to the user, but then the person is unable to know who messaged them.

What happens if the user does not turn off the location data? If the location data is off, then Tinder will remind them to turn it back on because if they do not, then they are unable to use the application. Although the purpose of the application is for people to meet others in their area, it gives others users more information about the user than they should. It seems a little sketchy knowing that a complete stranger you met lives one kilometer away from you. Worst case scenario, the person is a complete stalker or murderer who has tendencies to stalk people and wants to chop you up into tiny pieces. Tinder will not know that the person is a murderer or stalker and they would not inform other Tinder users of that information.

How can a Tinder user protect his/her personal information from being exploited? Tinder does try to take security measures to help safeguard our personal information from unauthorized access and disclosure; however, they make it clear that no system can be completely secure. Subsequently, they state that although they take steps to secure our information, they do not guarantee it and we should not expect that our personal information, chats, or other communications will always remain secure. This is completely inaccurate because as mentioned above, Tinder said they shared our information with third parties for their benefit and now they are warning us that our communications will not remain secure. Tinder states that we should take care of how we would handle and disclose our personal information and should avoid sending personal information through an insecure email due to many accounts of spam messages. It seems interesting that they tell us to be careful about not sharing our personal information, when in fact; they are doing the exact same thing to us. This way if we get unsolicited messages, hacked or stalked by certain people then the company cannot be held accountable for their actions. This violates principle 1 of PIPEDA, which talks about accountability where an organization is responsible for personal information under its control and shall designate an individual or individuals who are accountable for the organization's compliance.[12]

What is the information a person needs to provide about themselves while using Tinder? Tinder allows us to post information about ourselves and others while communicating with other users. Every post is governed by their Terms of Use and whenever we voluntarily disclose personal information on publicly-viewable pages, that information will be publicly available and can be collected and used by others. For example, if a person posts their email address on the website, they may receive unsolicited messages from people and some of those messages can be linked to viruses. Tinder cannot control who reads our posting or what other users may do with the information we voluntarily post, so Tinder encourages us to exercise discretion and caution with respect to our personal information. What is interesting to know is that Tinder does not monitor their users' photos, which concludes that as long as the person has "inappropriate" photos on Facebook, it can be posted on Tinder, and Tinder does nothing about it, which leads to my next issue about children's privacy.

---

[12] "PIPEDA and Your Practice a Privacy Handbook for Lawyers"

Children's privacy

Although Tinder is a general audience service, they restrict the use of their service to individuals under the age of 13. They do not knowingly collect, maintain, or use personal information from children under the age of 13, but what if the person is under the age of 13 and has access to Tinder? Since Tinder violates our privacy right, does it affect children who are underage? If Tinder is violating the right of a person who is not underage, then they are most definitely violating the right of a child, but here we are looking at the context of a child and there are rules and standards that are applied to children that may not be related to adults. If you are underage does PIPEDA's principle 3 about consent come into effect? Are children held to a higher standard? These questions all lead to invading the privacy right of a child and whether it is illegal or not? Every individual should have the right to consent to things that they are signing, but a 12-year old can click "I agree" and would not know what he/she is signing and this can lead to problems such as child pornography. It is common for the child's picture and information to be shared with other servers for "recordkeeping purposes" but, what do you do when a 30-year old is prying on a 12-

year old or a 13-year old child intentionally? On the other hand,

what if they do not know that the person is actually underage? This

is a perfect example of the Tyga case where he stated that he

messaged a girl to give her a modeling career, but instead it was

revealed that she was actually 14 years old.[13] With the new age of

technology, children are being exposed to sexually explicit content

and as children; they are unaware of what is right and what is wrong.

Children also do not know the difference between what is personal

or private information, in which they assume that the person they are

talking to online is a genuinely good person, but in reality, that

person could be using that information against the child and his/her

family.[14] Furthermore, this is how stalking a child and preying on

them works and by connecting with strangers online, sexual

offenders target online games or chat groups to coerce children to

send nude or partially clothed images, videos of themselves or make

them engage in sexual acts.[15] From previous experience and with

children whose parents do not monitor what their child is doing, it is

---

[13] Blair, Olivia. "Tyga: 14-year-old Girl Who 'received Messages from Kylie Jenner's Boyfriend' Hosts Press Conference."
[14] Department of Public Safety Victim Services.
[15] IBID.

easy to get caught up with strangers online who know the right things to say because we as children can be naive and believe whatever grown-ups tell us. Looking back to always accepting random strangers on Facebook, it makes me wonder if there is a way for the application to weave out people who you do not know and could possibly be a threat to you. Children can also lie about their age on Facebook, so they can lie about it on Tinder and get away with it. Tinder does not monitor our age, since it is connected to Facebook, so they are unaware how old a person is. Furthermore, the application age ranges from 18-55+, which means that anyone under 18 has no use for the application.

Visiting our Service from outside the United States

If someone decides to visit Tinder outside of the United States, then the person should be aware that their information may be transferred, stored, and processed in the United States where the servers are located and where the central database operates. By using this service, users are aware and agree that their information can be transferred to different areas and to all third parties associated with Tinder. PIPEDA will be discussed later on, but it is important to mention that although Tinder is located in the United States,

PIPEDA is not effective. This is a problem that we have to deal with in terms of privacy because many of the users' privacy in America or all over the world are not protected under PIPEDA. Furthermore, even though we have safeguards that protect our privacy, it does not mean that PIPEDA is actually effective.

No Rights of Third Parties

This Privacy Policy does not create rights to people that are enforceable by third parties or require disclosure of any personal information relating to users of the website. As mentioned before every third party has their own privacy policy. So what we do when we are not on Tinder does not comply with the application itself, but rather the third party websites that we are on and this means that we should take extra precaution.

Changes to this Privacy Policy

Since Tinder was created on September 15, 2012, they will occasionally update their privacy policy whenever they feel that it is necessary. When they post changes to this policy, they will revise the "last updated" date at the top of the page so users are aware. However, they do not provide their first privacy policy to look into and see what they changed about it. A question that keeps coming up is why did Tinder update their privacy policy? Tinder may have had to update its privacy policy due to legal cases or even because there was a problem with the application in which someone had to sue the company for damages that have been caused to a person. Tinder recommends that we check their service from time to time to inform ourselves of any changes in this privacy policy or any of their other policies. When Tinder uses the word inform, they are not stating that they will email us, but that we should take the initiative and do it ourselves.

PIPEDA

PIPEDA also known as The Personal Information Protection and Electronic Documents Act is a federal legislation that received royal assent on April 13, 2000, came into force on January 1, 2001and fully implemented on January 1, 2004.[16] While some provinces have passed their own privacy legislation, Ontario has not so PIPEDA applies here.[17] The bill was introduced by John Manley, the ministry of Industry.[18] PIPEDA includes 2 acts that were fused at the same time of introduction to the House of Commons.[19] The first

[16]Fortunato, Steven. "PIPEDA: How Are We Doing?
[17] IBID, Tutorial
[18]IBID, Tutorial

part deals with the privacy matter and the second part deals with the legal validation of most electronic communications (OPCC).[20] PIPEDA appointed the Office of the Privacy Commissioner of Canada to oversee its implementation and there are 10 principles to PIPEDA.[21] These principles include accountability, identifying purposes, consent, limiting collection, limiting use, disclosure and retention, accuracy, safeguard, openness, individual access, and challenging compliance.[22] Generally, PIPEDA does not seem to be effective because it is a very narrow legislation in terms of its privacy policy for users on certain applications. This means that technology keeps changing and PIPEDA needs to keep up with the changes because looking over it every 5 years or more does not guarantee that corporations are following what PIPEDA states in its act. Furthermore, the OPCC has very little enforcement powers under PIPEDA, which means that the OPCC lacks order making powers and is incapable of serving out fines for violators.[23]

---

[19] IBID, Tutorial
[20] PIPEDA and Your Practice a Privacy Handbook for Lawyers
[21] IBID.
[22] IBID.
[23] IBID.

The first principle of PIPEDA is accountability and we ask ourselves does the policy state who is held responsible and where do they stop? Tinder does not state who is responsible specifically, but it does talk about users being aware of sharing personal information or posting personal pictures online. Tinder tries not to be held accountable for anything that happens and the user is held accountable because Tinder states that we should be aware of what is on their privacy policy. The user should make sure to read the privacy policy to ensure our safety and knowledge of the application. A recent article was posted about how Tinder deleted everyone's matches and conversation. Instead of taking action, the first thing people saw was Tinder claiming that they are experiencing some issues at the moment where some users are not able to log in.[24] The company did not take the blame and tried to fix the glitch, but rather described to users that they are unable to do anything at the moment and that users should just sit back and wait until it comes back on.[25] This made users uneasy because nobody was doing anything

---

[24] Mullins, Jenna. "A Tinder Outage Accidentally Deleted Users' Matches and People Are PANICKING."
[25] IBID.

productive to get the system working again and the users felt hopeless because they could not do anything about it.

The second principle is identifying purposes which look at whether or not the policy states why it collects data? Does it outline reasons and do we think by not identifying it are users not swayed by it? The policy states that it collects data because it wants its users to have a better experience and enjoy their time. However, people are not swayed by this because even though the reason why the data is collected is stated, it implies that a person's safety is not taken care of since what we do online is saved and used for other purposes.

The third principle is consent which asks how is consent given to users? Who owns the application and who is it connected too? How much are we willing to give up and do we always have to consent to what the app is asking us? Users do not have to click on "I agree" but they consent through Facebook because when they authorize the application, hey are agreeing indirectly to all the terms and conditions. There is no formal consent, but by signing onto Facebook, we agree to the terms and conditions. Tinder is owned by Sean Rad, Jonathan Badean, Justin Mateen, Joe Munoz, Whitney Wolfe, Dinesh Morgan and Chris Gylczynski. We are willing to give up all our information, pictures, and private information without knowing it. We do not always have to consent, but Tinder informs us that we should always be up to date with their privacy policy.

In terms of consent, Tinder has 3 different forms of consent from the time you sign up until the time you deactivate your account which includes: explicit consent, implicit consent, and opt-out consent. Explicit consent – express or direct consent – means that an individual is presented with an option to agree or disagree with the collection, use, or disclosure of personal information.[26] For example, when a user is signing up for Tinder they are explicitly told what Tinder is offering them and what the code of conduct includes. Although Tinder may have other plans with our personal information, they cannot be held liable, since they can argue that what everything a user needs to know is on their privacy policy. Tinder cannot be blamed for a person's lack of understanding what the application is asking from a user. Explicit consent is usually required when clear, documentable consent is required, and the purposes for which it is being provided for is sensitive.[27] Explicit

---

[26] "Different Types of Consent - PrivacySense.net."
[27] IBID.

consent can be provided verbally or in writing.[28] Tinder also has implicit consent –deemed or indirect consent- which can mean a person voluntarily personal information for an organization to collect, use or disclose for purposes that would be considered obvious at the time.[29] For example, when we sign up for Tinder, we need to connect it to Facebook, which indicates that we are voluntarily giving up our personal information for Tinder to collect and share with whoever they want. This also means that if we want to use Tinder, we have to share our information on Facebook with them. The third consent that Tinder uses is opt-out consent – giving consent by not declining to give consent – means that an individual is given the option to decline consent.[30] For example, if an individual does not clearly decline consent, then consent is granted. Opt-out consent is usually done in writing, however, Tinder lets their user opt out of anything they do not feel comfortable with, but that could mean that the user may not be able to enjoy the services the application has to offer. Many organizations, especially websites,

---

[28] IBID.
[29] IBID.
[30] IBID.

use opt-out consent as a way to request permission to use our personal information for other purposes.[31]

The next principle is limiting use, disclosure, and retention which asks what are the problems with keeping certain information for a long period of time. There are many problems of keeping certain information private because not only does it keep a person safe, but a person can change over time. The information that we had about us a few years ago would have changed, which means what we like or our hobbies change over time. Furthermore, what we post online changes over time and what we thought was appropriate or funny back then is different from now. Tinder wants to make sure that their users are enjoying the experience, but in terms of listening to users' feedback or input, they do no such thing to protect or help out a concerned person about the application.

When looking at accuracy, we ask ourselves can who we portray online be who we really are? We cannot portray who we really are because people like to hide certain aspects of them. When we have secrets, it keeps people mysterious. How can we empower the law to protect us and does it really protect us? The law can

---

[31] IBID.

protect us in terms of keeping information private, but it does nothing to protect us because the corporation looks out for themselves and makes sure that they are making a profit.

Safeguards are another principle of PIPEDA and that is when personal information shall be protected by security safeguards appropriate to the sensitivity of the information. As discussed before, there are no safeguards and personal information is not protected. Tinder has told users should that they should take precaution to safeguard oneself from harm, but also be aware of whom they are sharing their information with so that they are safe online.

Openness discusses how an organization shall make information available to individual about policies and practices relating the management of persona information. Management of personal information is discussed very briefly in the privacy policy, but it does not go into detail in order to better assist the user in terms of understanding what Tinder is looking to get from them. What is on their policy is what a user sees and has to abide by the very general rules set out in Tinder's privacy policy.

Individual access is explained as upon an individual's request, an organization should make known to the individual the existence, use and disclosure of personal information and give access to it.[32] If a person challenges the accuracy or completeness of his or her personal information, the organization should amend the information where appropriate, which can involve correcting.[33] What Tinder fails to do is it does not share personal information of their user when requested and this is a problem because it violates the individual access principle. This is ironic because Tinder shares our information with other companies, but it will not share personal information with the person who actually requested it. It is then when we question, why is Tinder hiding our information from us? If other companies have the right to our personal information, then so should we. One would argue that Tinder may not want to share our personal information with us because people would then find flaws in their privacy policy and they would have to continuously amend it to fit the need of each individual. Furthermore, this would complicate the process of Tinder because it would not be running efficiently and the privacy policy would have to be continuously changing.

---

[32] "The 10 Privacy Principles of PIPEDA - PrivacySense.net."
[33] IBID.

Finally, challenging compliance states that the individual shall be able to challenge an organization's compliance on any of the privacy principles of PIPEDA.[34] This means that an organization must have procedures in place to receive and respond to complaints and inquiries and the procedures should be simple and easy to use.[35] In order to file a complaint about Tinder, you can only do so by going to their website and sending an email to their website or a person can email goprivacy@tinder.ca. Once an email is sent to Tinder, the person receives an email saying that the application has received the email and that someone will contact them shortly. It does not state how long this will take and when someone will contact them back, so the user is sitting there waiting and hoping that someone will contact them back. If this is a serious issue, then the person cannot wait for change to happen and they could be putting themselves in a terrible situation. Also, if an email was sent to Tinder about a problem and the user does not follow up on that email, they can ultimately forget about it and assume it is a waste of time. However, we cannot just put the blame on the user, but rather

---

[34] IBID.
[35] IBID.

Tinder as a company because whenever you decide to ask for anything related to your personal information then it is harder to know if anyone on the other end has actually received your email.

We have to question who the privacy violators include and what the necessary solutions are. The OPCC does not name the companies with complaints against them, even if they are repeat offenders, especially if it is online. The OPCC posts the findings of a particular case, however, they are only summaries and even the full findings were given to complaints are so narrow and limited that they are typically seen as useless.[36] An example, that is not related to Tinder, but can be connected to how the POCC does try to save corporations is PIAC v. Bell Mobility. The case is about how Bell was allowed to allege that the OPCC got the facts wrong and to provide a different version of facts in advance of the final findings without informing PIAC (Public Interest Advocate Center).[37] The question that was discussed was should there be a disclosure clause or should such a thing be left to courts only? Is it okay to give someone the benefit of the doubt or a pass on human error?[38] We

---

[36] Fortunato, Steven. "PIPEDA: How Are We Doing?"
[37] IBID, Tutorial.
[38] IBID, Tutorial.

have to be aware that corporations are looking out only for their best interest and by not exposing high profile cases to the public. As far as the public knows, these corporations have done nothing wrong. Additionally, if the public is unaware of what corporations such as Tinder were being sued for, then no one would step up or sue the company for damages that could have been caused due to privacy.

While Tinder refused or did not respond to my email about sending all my personal information to me, I had to take extra measures and contact the Ontario privacy commissioner, in which Karen Hale (Bilingual Communications Officer) stated that Tinder is actually a federal situation and I would need to contact the Privacy Commissioner of Canada as it oversees the Personal Information Protection and Electronic Documents Acts (PIPEDA), which covers private sector businesses in Ontario. It is crucial to mention that even though you get the Privacy Commissioner of Canada involved, it takes days to process and help you with your request. Although, people should not give up if they really want to pursue a corporation that will not give the user their private personal information when requested.

What is the point of having PIPEDA if it does nothing to protect individuals? PIPEDA gives us the illusion of choice and having rights, but it also makes us feel safe, although we have learned that people are not safe online.[39] People assume that they are safe, but in reality, our information is being retained and shared with other corporations for their own use to do whatever they want with it. Next, we need to understand who drafted PIPEDA and who did the act benefit? PIPEDA was drafted by major CEO's and corporations, in which the interest was presented, but it was drafted for CEO's and corporations and it does not look at the consumers privacy rights.[40] The stakeholders can include: businesses, government consumer advocacy groups, civil society and academia to hear their views on the strategic areas that pose the greatest threat to Canadians' privacy, and the areas in which the OPC could have the greatest positive impact.[41] Some of the stakeholders could be qualified in legislating for this law such as the government in terms of protecting citizens as well as advocacy groups because they can

---

[39] Mohmmadi, Behzad. "The Curated Web: There Is No Internet in the State of Nature." Tutorial
[40] IBID, Tutorial
[41] "Reports and Publications." Office of the Privacy Commissioner of Canada.

better assist the legislatures what the bill needs and how it can actually protect individuals.

Canada's PIPEDA and its enforcement mechanisms have many safeguards that could be implemented to protect the privacy of online users. These safeguards for Tinder can include: monitoring their users' photos, by making sure they do not upload photos that may seem inappropriate, in which Tinder is held accountable for their actions. Tinder should also safeguard their users' personal information by making sure that people are on a need to know basis, in which information should be provided to a person if they ever ask for it. Tinder can always ask for some sort of ID or they could have a phone number that people can call and talk too. It needs to be clear that the more sensitive the information is, the stronger the safeguards must be.[42] Although PIPEDA has safeguards to try and protect individuals from having their information exposed, it does very little in the long run. There should be solutions addressed about Tinder such as how users can access their personal information without being vulnerable to threats from outside of our virtual self. We are all human and we all make mistakes, but it is important to know who

---

[42]PIPEDA and Your Practice a Privacy Handbook for Lawyers

we are online and what we do does not define us a whole. The person we are online is just a piece of us that people are trying to get to know. Furthermore, people can pretend to be someone they are not online and who they are as a person is completely different.

While we know that Tinder does not take care of its users' privacy policy, it obviously means that the government does not either. This is known as free market government in which the government does not pry into peoples' privacy and corporations start competing with one another to prove to people who is offering the better service.[43] In a free market society, the government has a legitimate role in coordinating large projects for the common good such as national defense, the interstate road system aviation safety etc.[44] These are services which everyone relies upon and which, if they did not already exist, the public would eventually decide they would contribute to paying for to institute. When the government starts to meddle in the decisions made in the Free Market, efficiency and prosperity are reduced.[45] Previous efforts by governments to

---

[43] Behzad. "The Curated Web: There Is No Internet in the State of Nature." Tutorial
[44] "Free Market Questions."
[45] IBID.

take control of decisions that have had disastrous consequences, such as in the former Soviet Union.[46] It should not be the government's responsibility to make sure that what people are doing online is safe, but they can come up with stricter laws to implement and make sure that corporations follow these newly implemented rules. It is hard to argue whether or not a free market style government or an active government is the best approach because even though there would be deregulations and lack of restrictions on how information is shared between corporations, the government needs to have some input on how corporations are running their businesses. It has been proven that PIPEDA is not effective and by not repealing the bill or modifying it, corporations are following the same rules that were set out fifteen years ago. Also, the government should not be overseeing everything that corporations do, but rather making sure that corporations are not taking advantage of people and using their private information for their own benefits. This is known as a mixed economic system, where the corporations are free to do whatever they want, but the government can still get involved.[47]

---

[46] IBID.
[47] "Mixed Economic System Definition | Investopedia."

John Oliver in his clip *Encryption* spoke about how Encryption is fundamental in all our lives. Every time we log onto an internet service (Tinder, Facebook, Twitter) and send out our password gets protected using encryption code.[48] It can protect things that are important to us. It has a downside, ambiguous and impossible for law enforcement to gain access to certain information.[49] This can have and it is important for the government to make sure that they can have access to people's phones.[50] Apple's CEO Tim Cook spoke about how the government should not have access to our information, but this is just a way for corporations such as Apple to control what sort of access they can take from their users. John Oliver uses the metaphor of the government as our dad, in which if our dad asks us to help him with his phone we should be careful because if we help him once, we will be doing this fourteen times a day.[51] This explains how the government will continuously ask for corporations to infringe on rights of their users by accessing their personal information. The government should never have access to a

---

[48] Oliver, John. "Encryption." YouTube
[49] IBID, YouTube
[50] IBID, YouTube
[51] IBID, YouTube

person's personal information unless the person poses a threat or is involved in terrorist activities.

International Legislation

Privacy is a universal human right and there are several international accords related to privacy that serve as the foundation for international laws, policy frameworks, and international agreements throughout the world.[52] Similarly to the United Nations, the 47 member states of the Council of Europe have drafted several agreements to advance citizens' privacy rights as part of a broader commitment to cooperation and the development of human rights and fundamental freedoms.[53] The convention of the protection of individuals with regard to automatic processing of personal data is included in treaty number 108.[54] This convention protects individuals against the abuses which may accompany the collection and processing of personal data and it provides guarantees in relation to the collection and processing of personal data, it outlaws the processing of "sensitive" data on a person's race, politics, health,

---

[52] "International Privacy Standards."
[53] IBID.
[54] "Convention for the Protection of Individuals with Regard to Automatic Processing of Personal Data."

Odisho 51

religion, sexual life, criminal record, etc., in the absence of proper legal safeguards."[55] The convention also allows the individual's right to know that information is stored on him or her and, if necessary, to have it corrected.[56] Under the UN deceleration of human rights, privacy is a fundamental human right, in which it underpins human dignity and other key values such as freedom of association and freedom of speech.[57] Every country around the world recognizes the right to privacy in their constitutions. In many of the countries where privacy is not explicitly recognized in the Constitution, such as the United States, Ireland, and India, the courts have found that right in other provisions.[58] In many countries, international agreements that recognize privacy rights such as the International Covenant on Civil and Political Rights or the European Convention on Human Rights have been adopted into law.[59] The reason many countries adopted such a law was to remedy past injustices, such as Central Europe, south America, and south Africa, in which privacy violations occurred under previous authoritarian regimes.[60] It was also to

---

[55] IBID.
[56] IBID.
[57] "Privacy and Human Rights - Overview."
[58] IBID.
[59] IBID.

promote electronic commerce in which countries such as Asia, but also Canada developed or are currently developing laws in an effort to promote electronic commerce.[61] These countries recognize consumers are uneasy with their personal information being sent worldwide.[62] Privacy laws are being introduced as part of a package of laws intended to facilitate electronic commerce by setting up uniform rules.[63] Finally, it is to ensure that laws are consistent with Pan-European laws, in which most countries in Central and Eastern Europe are adopting new laws based on the Council of Europe Convention and the European data protection Directive.[64] Many of these countries hope to join the European Union in the near future. Countries in other regions, such as Canada, are adopting new laws to ensure that trade will not be affected by the requirements of the EU Directive.[65]

In January 2012, the European Commission proposed a comprehensive reform of data protection rules in the EU.[66] The

---

[60] IBID.
[61] IBID.
[62] IBID.
[63] IBID.
[64] IBID.
[65] IBID.
[66] "Protection of Personal Data."

object of this new set of rules is to give citizens back control over of their personal data and to simplify the regulatory environment for business.[67] The data protection reform is a key enabler of the digital single market which the commission has prioritized. The reform will allow European citizens and businesses to fully benefit from the digital economy.[68] If Canada had laws - aside from what PIPEDA is stating - to give citizens back control over their personal data and to simply regulate the environment for business, then consumers are able to regulate what kind of information is being shared and with whom it is shared. Furthermore, this gives consumers control over their privacy information so that we do not expose ourselves to the wrong people.

Under European Union (EU) law, personal data can only be gathered legally under strict conditions, for a legitimate purpose.[69] Furthermore, persons' or organizations' which collect and manage your personal information must be protected from misuse and must respect certain rights of the data owners which are guaranteed by EU law.[70] Every day within the EU, businesses, public authorities and

---

[67] IBID.
[68] IBID.
[69] IBID.

individuals transfer vast amounts of personal data across borders.[71] Conflicting data protection rules in different countries would disrupt international exchanges.[72] Individuals might also be unwilling to transfer personal data abroad if they were uncertain about the level of protection in other countries.[73] Therefore, common EU rules have been established to ensure that your personal data enjoys a high standard of protection everywhere in the EU.[74] You have the right to complain and obtain redress if your data is misused anywhere within the EU.[75] The EU's Data Protection Directive also foresees specific rules for the transfer of personal data outside the EU to ensure the best possible protection of your data when it is exported abroad.[76]

The charter brings together all the rights previously found in a variety of legislative instruments such as international and EU laws, as well as International Conventions from the council of Europe, the United Nations, and the International Labour Organisation.[77] By making fundamental rights clearer and more

---

[70] IBID.
[71] IBID.
[72] IBID.
[73] IBID.
[74] IBID.
[75] IBID.
[76] IBID.
[77] "EUR-Lex Access to European Union Law."

visible, it creates legal certainty with the EU.[78] The Charter of

Fundamental Rights contains a preamble and 54 articles, grouped

into seven chapters, which includes: dignity, freedoms, equality,

solidarity, citizens' rights, justice, and general provisions.[79] Dignity

is the human right, which includes the right to life, the right to the

integrity of the person, prohibition of torture and inhuman or

degrading treatment or punishment, prohibition of slavery and forced

labor.[80] Freedoms is the right to liberty and security, respect for

private and family life, protection of personal data, the right to marry

and found a family, freedom of thought, conscience and religion,

freedom of expression, and information, freedom of assembly and

association, freedom of the arts and sciences, the right to education,

freedom to choose an occupation and the right to engage in work,

freedom to conduct a business, the right to property, the right to

asylum, protection in the event of removal, expulsion or extradition.[81]

Equality looks at the equality before the law, non-discrimination,

cultural, religious and linguistic diversity, equality between men and

---

[78] IBID.
[79] IBID.
[80] IBID.
[81] IBID.

women, the rights of the child, the rights of the elderly, and

integration of persons with disabilities.[82] Solidarity is when the

workers' right to information and consultation within the

undertaking, the right of collective bargaining and action, the right of

access to placement services, protection in the event of unjustified

dismissal, fair and just working conditions, prohibition of child

labour and protection of young people at work, family and

professional life, social security and social assistance, health care,

access to services of general economic interest, environmental

protection, consumer protection.[83] "Citizens' rights include the right

to vote and stand as a candidate in elections to the European

Parliament and at municipal elections, the right to good

administration, the right of access to documents, European

Ombudsman, the right to petition, freedom of movement and

residence, diplomatic and consular protection."[84] Justice is the right

to an effective remedy and a fair trial, presumption of innocence and

the right of defense, principles of legality and proportionality of

---

[82] IBID.
[83] IBID.
[84] IBID.

criminal offenses and penalties, the right not to be tried or punished twice in criminal proceedings for the same criminal offense.[85]

Conclusion

Cases such as the case of Gable Tostee (2014),[86] and the Kelly McCarthy case (2014)[87] discuss how Tinder's privacy policy is actually ineffective in terms of keeping people's personal information private and whether certain changes such as reviewing customer complaints or removing certain aspects like not connecting to Facebook the moment we sign in is effective. Also, I socially deconstructed cases that Tinder had been sued because they were not following its privacy policy, but rather tricking people into believing that their information was safeguarded. These class action lawsuits range from sexual assault to the new fees that the application has asked people to use. Furthermore, as previously mentioned the policy is not compliant with domestic laws or international laws and treaties regarding privacy. Furthermore, Tinder is not safe and

---

[85] IBID.
[86] Moir, Jo. "Tinder Helps Build Case."
[87] McCarthy, Kelly. "Someone Used My Photo to Create a Fake Tinder Account, And It Could Happen to You."

people are being blindsided by the applications features to really

understand what is going on.

Work Cited

Blair, Olivia. "Tyga: 14-year-old Girl Who 'received Messages from Kylie Jenner's Boyfriend' Hosts Press Conference." *The Independent*. Independent Digital News and Media, 05 Jan. 2015. Web. 03 Feb. 2016.

"Convention for the Protection of Individuals with Regard to Automatic Processing of Personal Data." *Treaty Office*. Web. 17 Mar. 2016.

Department of Public Safety Victim Services. *Child Internet Safety: A Guide for Parents, Caregivers, Teachers and Others Who Work with Children and Youth*. Fredericton: Department of Public Safety Victim Services, 2015. Mar. 2015. Web. 03 Feb. 2016.

"Different Types of Consent - PrivacySense.net." *PrivacySensenet*. 09 July 2015. Web. 11 Mar. 2016.

Epstein, Sue. "Convicted Suitcase Killer Melanie McGuire Is Investigating If Her Lawyer Was on Drugs during Her 2007

Trial." *NJ.com New Jersey*. 10 July 2014. Web. 10 Feb. 2016.

EUR-Lex Access to European Union Law." *EUR-Lex*. Web. 18 Mar. 2016.

Free Market Questions. (n.d.). Retrieved March 20, 2016, from http://www.freemarketquestions.org/What_is_the_role_of_go vernment_in_the_free_market.htm

Fortunato, Steven. "PIPEDA: How Are We Doing?" Class 15. Vari Hall, Toronto. 02 Feb. 2016. Tutorial.

"International Privacy Standards." *Electronic Frontier Foundation*. Web. 17 Mar. 2016.

Kobzar, Olena. "Introducing the Data Double." Class 10. Vari Hall, Toronto. 02 Feb. 2016. Lecture.

Kobzar, Olena. "Secrets." Class 11. Vari Hall, Toronto. 19 Nov. 2015. Lecture.

Kobzar, Olena. "Privacy Law in Canada." Class 14. Vari Hall, Toronto. 02 Feb. 2016. Lecture.

McCarthy, Kelly. "Someone Used My Photo To Create A Fake Tinder Account, And It Could Happen To You." *Thought Catalog*. Dec.-Jan. 2014. Web. 03 Feb. 2016.

"Mixed Economic System Definition | Investopedia." *Investopedia*.

    2010. Web. 20 Mar. 2016.

Mohmmadi, Behzad. "The Curated Web: There Is No Internet in the

    State of Nature." Tutorial #23. Vari Hall, Toronto. 19 Mar.

    2016. Lecture.

Moir, Jo. "Tinder Helps Build Case." *Stuff*. 29 Nov. 2014. Web. 10

    Feb. 2016.

Mullins, Jenna. "A Tinder Outage Accidentally Deleted Users'

    Matches and People Are PANICKING." Eonline 14 Mar.

    2016. Print.

Oliver, John. "Encryption." *Last Week Tonight with John Oliver*.

    HBO/YouTube. 13 Mar. 2016. Television.

"PIPEDA and Your Practice a Privacy Handbook for Lawyers."

    Office of the Privacy Commissioner of Canada. Web. 03 Feb.

    2016.

"Privacy and Human Rights - Overview." *Privacy and Human

    Rights - Overview*. Web. 19 Mar. 2016.

"Protection of Personal Data." - *European Commission*. Web. 17

    Mar. 2016.

"Reports and Publications." *Office of the Privacy Commissioner of Canada*. Government of Canada. Web. 19 Mar. 2016.

"Tinder - Any Swipe Can Change Your Life." *Tinder*. 31 July 2015. Web. 03 Feb. 2016.

"The 10 Privacy Principles of PIPEDA - PrivacySense.net." *PrivacySensenet*. 2015. Web. 13 Mar. 2016.

"The Universal Declaration of Human Rights | United Nations." *UN News Center*. UN. Web. 18 Mar. 2016.

"What Are Cookies? Computer Cookies Explained." *What Are Cookies*. Web. 03 Feb. 2016.

www.ingramcontent.com/pod-product-compliance
Lightning Source LLC
LaVergne TN
LVHW012315070326
832902LV00001BA/19